HOW TO BE A PASTOR
IN A MAD, MOD WORLD

HOW TO BE A
Pastor in a Mad, Mod World

by Nathanael M. Guptill

THE BETHANY PRESS
ST. LOUIS, MISSOURI

Contents

1.

The Mad, Mod World Is the Only One We've Got

WHAT EXCUSE can one have for writing another book about our changing modern world and the relationship of the ministry (if any) to it? Surely more already has been written on this subject than anybody can possibly read. But I have been waiting in vain for somebody to say what will be said in the following pages; and since it appears that no one else is likely to say it, I had better —if only, as they say, "for my own amusement."

The books already written fall into a few identifiable categories:

1. Those which describe the church as moribund and irrelevant and the ministry as hopelessly corrupt,

and leave one with the feeling that if he can possibly do so it would be wise to desert the foundering ship before it disappears beneath the waves.

2. Those which describe the sins of American culture and the identification of the clergy with those sins in such a way that we have a choice between espousing reform programs that partake of the stuff of LSD visions or wallowing forever in hopeless and abject guilt.

3. The "Great Time to Be Alive" type books which speak with almost hysterical joy about a new world aborning that will be devoid of anything we presently enjoy, and adopt as their major premise the notion that any of the religious beliefs on which we have based our lives are patently incredible.

4. The "Waiting for Godot" books which describe human existence in terms of meaninglessness and man's plight as devoid of hope.

I do not want to seem to be knocking these books. It's just that they do not offer much help to me in attacking my day-to-day problems. I am free to admit that their dire prophecies may be true and that the world I know may come crashing to an end any minute. This will perhaps change the timetable of my life but not its ultimate fate, which I know too well already.

What we must have is some help in deciding what to do with our lives in the relatively short time any of us has left (even supposing that medical science will keep our children alive a hundred years or more).

What I shall try to say in the following pages is:

First, this mad, mod world is the only one we've got. It is not really a great deal more perilous than Europe in the time of the Black Death, and its people on the whole have more moral awareness than the human race of a few centuries ago. But it is a great deal different from any world that mankind has ever known before and it is changing fast enough to make our heads spin. If we are going to do any good or have any fun, it has to be in this world; so questions as to whether this world is better or worse than any other are academic.

Second, those of us who are in the parish ministry or are contemplating entering the parish ministry have to know the answers to two questions if we are to continue on this vocational path:

- Is it possible to maintain one's integrity while serving as a parish minister?
- Is it possible to succeed in attaining some of one's goals in this calling without being unfaithful to the gospel of Christ?

These two questions are related to each other in ways we shall see. They are very much on the minds of many pastors. It is my conviction that for some pastors the answer to these questions is no. For others—indeed, for many—the answer is yes. It is possible to succeed, to be faithful, and to maintain as much integrity as is possible for any sinful human in the parish ministry.

If these questions seem to be put in a negative form, it is because negative thinking is the only kind done in many places today. But it can be put positively.

A dozen years ago I wrote a book called *Young Man, You're Wanted,* urging young men to enter the parish ministry. More than twenty thousand copies of that paperback are around somewhere, probably because they were given away by a theological seminary and a denominational department of the ministry. In it I said that the parish ministry is the most important (that was before the word *relevant* was invented or I would have used it), the most exciting, and the most personally rewarding vocation to which one could give himself. Nothing in the years since the book was written has caused me to alter that opinion.

There are things one now has to add to the story. The world is madder and modder than it was in the fifties. It is tremendously frustrating, tremendously dangerous, and all of us are vulnerable both to temptation and to danger. But that is true of businessmen, teachers, college presidents, politicians, and just about everybody else. That makes our world a good deal less comfortable than it was, and there are more unpleasant possibilities every day.

Nevertheless, as one old pro in the ministry said to me not long ago, "I guess people need a minister today just about as much as they need anybody, maybe more." That is why I still stick by my earlier conclusion—that the call to the parish ministry is more important than ever before.

2.

We Helped to Make It Both Mad and Mod

WE HAVE troubles in the ministry today that partake of the same kind of troubles everyone else has: the dislocations caused by the rapid growth of technology, the mobility of population that knocks the props out from under many people, the fears that war and the possibilities of more and greater wars plant in hearts already bewildered and rootless. Even the temptations and sweet-sour joys of affluence make for stresses and strains that are hard for the human psyche to bear.

In the midst of the mad, mod world, bruised and beaten by the rat race of competition, anxious about the future, one goes to his church to find a world that has not changed, a fellowship in which beliefs are eternal and hope is the coin of the realm. What does he find? Jazz is replacing Bach (and he was just getting used to Bach). The communion table has casters on it so that it can stand against the wall or in the middle of the chancel or sometimes down in the middle of the aisle. The minister, like the doctor, has abandoned house calls because he is too busy encouraging the employees of his parishioners to strike to engage in such trivia. And good old Matthew, Mark, Luke, and John, who somehow had just begun to make sense, are now set aside for people like Bultmann and Bonhoeffer and Cox and Marshall McLuhan.

How come?

The clergy and the church have had much to do with the turmoil of the world. Often without desiring it or fully understanding it, we have opened the sluice gates and let out forces that have gone farther and faster and in different directions than we expected. Let's itemize a few for identification:

1. Christianity has preached hope to the poor, and they have risen up to cash in all the promissory notes of two thousand years by demanding the substance of the things they have hoped for.

2. Christianity has preached against the materialistic presuppositions of the modern world and has begotten a race that questions all presuppositions and insists on reexamining all beliefs, Christian or otherwise.

3. Christianity since its beginning has brought war into question as a proper means of settling quarrels between nations and now finds in our country a

new kind of secular pacifist who would abandon all responsibility for maintaining order by force—within the nation or among nations.

4. Christianity has preached the higher righteousness of love above the letter of the law and now confronts a "new morality" devoid of any norms or lasting guides to correct conduct.

5. Christianity has maintained always that a man must obey God first and the government second, but now contends with a philosophy that would overthrow both God and Caesar, taking us back to the good old days described in the Book of Judges during which "there was no king in Israel; every man did what was right in his own eyes."

6. Christianity has preached a God of change who " 'make[s] all things new' " and has given encouragement to a generation of people who worship change for its own sake and seem to desire a world in which the children run the homes, the pupils run the schools, the convicts run the prisons, the poor administer relief, and the laity run the church!

How do we as pastors cope with such a world and church? Like everyone else, we are troubled and confused more often than we might have been in a world that was neither as mad nor as mod as this one. Some of us are casualties and are defeated by forces too great for us to handle and by problems too great for us to understand, let alone solve.

Here again I think classification of the various kinds of response would be helpful. My job description states that I am to be "pastor to the ministers, and fraternal counselor to all the churches" in a conference which includes just under 300 churches and nearly 350 ordained ministers. In this capacity I listen to pastors for many hours every working week, and, in negotiating with grievance committees, pastoral committees, and other lay groups, I have occasion to hear from the people in the pews as well. Following are some of the more common types of pastors I meet:

Common or garden variety. He is the backbone of the church. In spite of all the stresses of modern life, it is still true that of all professional groups the best life expectancy is in a category called "clergy, Protestant, American." His children go farther in education (in spite of low incomes), get into *Who's Who* more often, and have fewer problems as a tribe than other children. He gives away a greater percentage of his income than a person in any other group of people except Seventh-day Adventists. Somehow he makes his peace with reality and often enjoys his work inordinately. All of this is in spite of the increasing incidence of adultery, emotional disease, professional failure, and just plain unhappiness among those around him.

The casualty. It came to me as a great shock while I was director of a denominational department of the ministry a decade ago that it is possible to fail in the ministry just as it is in any other profession. A casualty is one who leaves the ministry involuntarily. Sometimes it is due to the much-publicized "maceration" he gets in his job. Greater and greater demands are made on him by his people, by the books he reads, by his denominational promotional agencies, and by his conscience until he becomes torn asunder and either succumbs to mental illness or is simply paralyzed and unable to do anything because he is attempting so much. Others fail because of inability to work with people, or other incompetency. Some exit via the old route marked "moral turpitude." The most to be regretted are those failures caused because a man is chewed up spiritually by a church full of small, mean, vengeful people who torment him until he becomes sour on the whole enterprise and then fire him after making him unfit for future service.

The dropout. This is usually a young pastor (under forty), but sometimes he can be an older one who simply comes to the conclusion that the pastoral ministry is not for him. Sometimes it is merely a matter of faulty expectations. The young minister comes into town expecting to turn his congregation into gung ho social activists and devoted students of theology the first year. This doesn't happen—so he quits. There is usually a ritual of "shaking off the dust from his feet" before leaving. More often a minister drops out because of a dearth of the kinds of interests and gifts needed for the pastorate.

Whatever the reasons, the dropout usually leaves out of frustration and boredom. He finds himself unable to do what he thinks is important and importuned to do what he thinks is unimportant; so he seeks another profession in which he can get paid for doing what he really does want to do with his life. There are theological and ecclesiastical overtones to this process that will be noted in a later chapter.

The cop-out (not to be confused with the dropout). In biblical times this type was known as the "hireling prophet." He was paid to tell people what they wanted to hear about God's purposes. The cop-out sometimes is not tuned in to God at all. Sometimes he is. But his preaching and teaching are calculated to make his parishioners happy. This used to be easier than it is now. Some of the laity these days are happy enough without any help, and they want their pastors to help them make other church members unhappy by stirring up their consciences and warning them of moral dangers. So they are likely to bug their cop-out pastors almost as much as their square Christian brothers bug the dropouts.

The timeserver. This pastor is really a kind of casualty. Usually he went into the ministry with a great deal of joy and idealism, but for one reason or another the joy has gone from it. Sometimes it is because he does not really believe in God or his Son Jesus Christ anymore. Sometimes he has become so harried by trying to reconcile the doers and the prayers and the backsliders, and by trying unsuccessfully to please them all, that, like the proverbial sexton in the familiar story, he "just throws his mind into neutral and goes where he's pushed." Often he is a pastor caught in a church he has served too long and unable to move without taking such a cut in salary as to endanger the education of his children. As a result, he goes on without zest or enthusiasm, working out his time until retirement or until the church eases him out of his job (usually clumsily and with great pain for all concerned). Sometimes after this happens he will take a new lease on life in a smaller church and have a late burst of creative ministry; but often not.

I know and love all these people I have described because at various times I have been or have wanted to be each one of them. I guess all pastors at one time or another have felt like joining Elijah under the juniper tree or Jonah under the gourd or Jesus in Gethsemane. But these are not places where one can stay very long.

We have to go somewhere, and for us there is no place to go but the mad, mod world of the last third of the twentieth century.

Of course, there hovers over all our discussion the question of whether or not there will be a church in America in the 1980s like that we now know, or whether organized Christianity will be reduced to a quaint, antiquarian enterprise like the present churches of England and northern Europe. I remember my college roommate saying to me in 1938, "Don't you think the church has about outlived its usefulness?" This seemed to be the popular opinion on campus at that time in history. After a spurt of growth and visible vitality following World War II, we are now almost back where we were in 1938 and the students are once more asking the same question, "Don't you think the church has about had it?"

There are some interesting contrasts, however, between attitudes of present students and those of their parents thirty years ago. Today, although there is not a great deal of enthusiasm for organized churches (as indeed there has hardly ever been on college campuses), there is a great deal of interest in courses in religion. This generation of college graduates is going to know more about the content of Christian thought than any preceding generation in this century. And the clergy on campus are often mixed up "where the action is" in advocating and promoting leftward causes of all kinds, whatever that means for good or ill (and it is both good and ill).

For whatever help it may be, a Gallup poll reports that 57 percent of the people think the church is going downhill, whereas a decade ago only 17 percent thought this. I suspect that we sometimes mistake public opinion polls for reports of fact rather than opinion, and it may be that there is no more evil substance in the latter poll than there was good substance in the prior one. After all, if there is anything to the Christian enterprise, it is God who will decide its fate and not Mr. Gallup (who, by the way, would be the first to agree with this).

These points are more relevant to the young person contemplating the ministry than to those of us who have burned our bridges and are committed to it, but they have to be on our minds.

However, there are other things to consider about the current scene. Certainly, there has never before been a time in which religious news commanded the attention it receives today; there never has been a time when Christians—from the Roman Catholics on the right to the Quakers on the left—have been in serious conversation and cooperative endeavor as they are at this moment. And if it is of any comfort, even Marshall McLuhan affirms that the new age of involvement will see a great upsurge of interest in religion (even if not of religious institutions).

It is clear that pastors and the church have had a hand in making our mad, mod world what it is. It also is clear that religion, in spite of perennial predictions to the contrary, is likely to be here for some time.

This still leaves moot the question as to whether the parish ministry is a role in which one can have hopes of making a significant mark on the world, while at the same time remaining spiritually in one piece. We shall answer that question in the affirmative before we are finished.

3.

Success and Faithfulness—The Dilemma of Church and Minister

THE QUESTION that causes more hang-ups than any other in church and ministry is that of success and faithfulness. Usually it comes out as success *versus* faithfulness. Indeed, one almost hesitates to talk about success at all because it is so often identified as the opposite of faithfulness. But the desire to succeed in fulfilling one's purposes in life is so basic that it cannot be ignored. Even men in monastic orders who take vows of poverty, chastity, and obedience do not promise never to succeed.

The word *success* needs to be defined and rehabilitated before it can be used in the context of this discussion. There is a big fat idol in the New Testament called "Mammon," the object of devotion of all who sell out the human race and live for themselves alone. Today, the name of that idol is SUCCESS. The worship of this idol symbolizes everything phony, shallow, empty, and inhuman about our culture. The cult of the beautiful people described in TV commercials who consume cosmetics, beer, cigarettes, soap, and crunchy breakfast food, who wear smart clothes, drive flashy cars, and "get ahead" in life is the great false religion of our day. A great many Christians and a great many pastors are secret adherents of this religion, but few will admit it; and many are torn apart inside because, although they profess a slushy form of Christianity, they know that down deep they really want more than anything else to be young, rich, beautiful, strong, and sexy.

We have to take the word *success* out of that context and consider its fundamental meaning, which is to do what one wants to do. We must have a word to describe the personal fulfillment that every human being who does not opt out of life altogether must seek if he is to maintain either his sanity or his integrity. The only word that comes near carrying this meaning is *success,* even if the sound of the word brings on nausea and blurred vision.

For instance, a hippie can reject Victorian morality, accumulation of wealth, personal cleanliness, and all other generally accepted goals of the culture he has left behind; but he cannot get away from the need to succeed. He requires and strives for the approval of other hippies, the freedom to "do his thing," and some sense of inner wholeness either chemically or spiritually achieved—and in this striving he is unsuccessful or successful. What is more, his personal happiness is related to success or lack of it.

So it is in every human endeavor (because to the human, to live is to try). Even the rejection of success is a venture that either succeeds or fails. The Trappist monk who lives in silence strives harder than most to achieve his goals. I am reminded of Brother Juniper, the cartoon character, who was given a gold medal for being the most humble monk in the monastery but had to return it when he insisted on wearing it.

What I am trying to describe finds its deepest expression in one of the last words of Christ on the cross, " 'It is finished.' " It is a word that might have been used by Raphael after signing his name to a completed work of art, or by Beethoven after sending a sonata off to the publishers. The task of salvation for mankind which Christ had been born and called to do was finished. He succeeded as no man ever did before or since. When purpose and accomplishment match, then life is worth living. And the greater and nobler the purpose and the closer one comes to achievement, the more worth living life is.

This is an area in which ministers have a great deal of trouble. I know a famous preacher and president of a seminary who collects and repairs clocks for a hobby. He says that he does it because he feels the need to succeed at something; he finds fixing people such a frustrating business. The goals of the pastor are likely to be ultimate rather than proximate and therefore unachievable in this life.

The official personnel record of pastors prepared by the denomination to which I belong includes statements by each pastor as to what the goals of his ministry are and what successes he can point to in his ministry. One pastor said, "The goals of my ministry are the salvation of mankind and the coming of God's kingdom on this earth." When reciting his accomplishments on the way to achieving these goals, he boasted, "We have black-topped the parking lot of the church and redecorated the inside of the parsonage from top to bottom." This minister had no difficulty in seeing the relationship between his proximate and ultimate goals, and thus he saw himself as a great success. But many pastors find difficulty in this which the simpler thought lines of a more naïve generation did not encounter.

A pastor (whom I would rate as excellent in his profession) attended a clinical training quarter at a mental hospital under the direction of a very competent teaching chaplain. In reporting to me, the chaplain gave him high marks for performance and learning in all the things he tried to do. But he expressed concern that this pastor was depressed and harried because he could not bring himself to enjoy his successes.

Here was a graduate of an Ivy League seminary, beloved pastor of an enthusiastic congregation of above-average size. He had led the congregation in selling an outdated downtown building and moving to a more suitable site where the members lived. They had responded to his leadership by giving many hundreds of thousands of dollars of their money to build the buildings necessary to effect the move, by turning out hour after hour to work on the buildings with their own hands, and by participating wholeheartedly in the services of worship and the programs of education and fellowship conducted by the church. The Junior Chamber of Commerce chose this pastor as "young man of the year," and he is universally admired not only by his own people but by his fellow ministers.

All of this is not what he needs to accept and appreciate himself. He has been led to believe that he must see visible spiritual change in people's lives, that he must have victories in politics which change the community for the better, and that he must get his people head over heels in adult education before he will be doing his job to his own satisfaction.

This particular man loves people so much that he keeps on trying to help them as well as he can without the kind of self-satisfaction he would like to have. But he lives out his days in an uneasy state of armed truce with his conscience.

There are many causes for frustration due to lack of success in the life of a pastor. Some have to do with the low visibility of the real victories he achieves. Many come from differences of opinion between pastor and people about the main business of the church. Some arise out of special problems having to do with the madness and modness of our world.

For instance, take the great disparity between the expectations of pastors and those of congregations in the small churches likely to be served by new seminary graduates.

First, who is this new graduate seeking placement in his first church? Seventeen percent of those who enter seminaries today intend to become pastors (this varies from school to school, but the overall figure will stand up). By the time they graduate the 17 percent has been increased to about 25 percent who really want to be pastors. Fifty percent continue their education after seminary or enter some "ministry outside the organized church." This means that 25 percent of the total graduating class, or 50 percent of those who enter the pastorate, do not really want to be there. For a distressing number it is either the pastorate or military service.

At any rate, they have not found the "exciting new form of ministry" for which they prepared, or at least nobody wants to pay them to perform it; so they take the lesser evil. "I'll give the residential church a try," they say. They have been warned not to get caught in the rat race of silver teas and bean suppers, not to waste their time calling on old ladies, not to neglect their studies, and to be sure to confront their congregations with the demands of the gospel—which usually means telling them they are a bunch of middle-class white racists who had better become something else quickly or incur the displeasure of the new minister. This picture is not accurate with respect to the one out of two young pastors who entered the pastorate from choice, but for the other half, at least from my vantage point, it is not greatly exaggerated.

This young Savonarola comes to town, and what is expected of him? All the people in his congregation want a minister who will (1) preach in such a way as to convince them that life is worth living in spite of pain and failure and death; (2) conduct worship in a sincere and emotionally satisfying manner; (3) care for young and old in a personal way that is helpful; and (4) furnish leadership to programs of organization in the church that will attract other people to join it and help in paying the bills.

In addition, many want and all expect a ministry that (1) sets high and demanding ethical goals for the individual and for the family; (2) shows how lay vocations can be sacred ministries; and (3) leads in individual and collective efforts to improve the community, local and worldwide.

It really is not necessary to draw a picture of what happens when the union takes place. The minister thinks the congregation is hopelessly entangled in meaningless and fruitless pursuits. "Of what possible benefit can church membership be to a person?" one young pastor asked the church members who were paying his salary. It is not altogether surprising that the people become convinced that the pastor is accepting their money under false pretenses. Soon the pastor is making regular visits to a psychiatrist, the church is split into factions that may hate each other for a generation, and the whole enterprise is smothered in confusion.

The picture that comes to my mind as I think of these situations is that of the TV commercial in which the bright young housewife exclaims in exasperation, "What's a mother to do?" That is the feeling, and it will take more than some miracle soap powder or breakfast food to solve this problem. It will take honesty, some kind of reasonableness, a good deal of openness and tolerance, and the rare mixture of steadfastness and patience that is indispensable for survival as a pastor today.

When there is a clear-cut conflict between success and faithfulness, there is no question. Faithfulness wins. Indeed, faithfulness to the Christian commitment must be the ultimate goal; to be unfaithful is to be unsuccessful.

The first example of this kind of situation that comes to mind is that of a fine man with a Ph.D. who became a pastor when he could not get a teaching position. His vocation was to effect social change, and his understanding of the meaning of the Christian message today was that this must be primary on the agenda of the church. His preaching, his community leadership, his teaching, and his personal life were wholeheartedly dedicated to these goals. In his church about 20 percent thought he was God; about 20 percent thought he was the devil; and the rest either were uninterested or stuck it out because of loyalty to the church.

This caused a painful situation which lasted the better part of a decade. Some members were so threatened by the pastor's activities or so angry at his teaching (with which they disagreed) that they hounded him constantly. Attendance fell off, and many withheld their pledges. The pastor's stomach was upset, his wife was upset, and all his friends were upset. This is not to say that the situation had no good in it. A considerable number of people in the church became excited about the social implications of the Christian religion and became active in numerous programs for community betterment and social justice. But in the church the situation could not last forever.

Finally there was a church meeting at which the pastor received a vote of confidence, 118 to 110. Not long afterward he resigned and ultimately obtained a job with a state agency whose assignment it is to help people of minority groups achieve their civil rights and obtain employment, housing, and other benefits.

Now he is paid and praised for doing the things that got him into a peck of trouble while he was a pastor. He has found outside the pastorate the combination of vocational integrity, the sense of being faithful to his convictions, and the opportunity for some success in achieving proximate goals.

There will be those who, viewing this situation, will say that the church deserved to die because it rejected this minister; that the minister was being unfaithful in resigning until he was thrown out bodily or nailed to a tree; that this is really the whole story about the church of our day—a final proof of its "irrelevance."

Those who take this point of view would doubtless espouse the popular stereotype of the church's condition which says that if the church is growing in the "2 M's" (members and money), if its real estate is well kept up, its organizational life busy and well supported, and its sanctuary full on Sunday mornings with singing, praying people who seem to like one another, then the church must be in the complete control of Satan. But, on the other hand, if the membership is falling, if financial support is being withheld, if half the congregation hates the other half, and if the peeled paint hangs loosely from the clapboards of the meetinghouse, then there must be spiritual vitality of a high order present. If this were true, I would make two comments: (1) There are some evidences of this kind of vitality in all churches; and (2) I have never known a pastor or a church that could endure this kind of spiritual vitality very long after it reached maximum voltage.

Like all stereotypes, this one needs to be examined. It is accurate in one respect: When the hard truth of Christ's gospel is preached to people, it can make them hurt or angry or frightened. Jesus' friends told him one day that the Pharisees were offended by his words. The Pharisees are still offended. But after this has been acknowledged, it must be said that there are a great many more reasons for bad organizational health in a church than faithfulness to the Master. And faithfulness can show itself in increased membership, larger budgets, and more visible involvement of people in the church's life.

Sometimes a church can die of boredom when a pastor talks over the people's heads about matters that do not concern them. It does no good to be relevant to the "great issues of the day" if one is irrelevant to the people to whom he is talking. A certain denomination set apart a fund to help ministers who were in trouble with their congregations because of the race problem. Thirty-two ministers received help from this fund. I asked the administrator how many of these ministers would have been in trouble if there had been no civil rights struggle. He replied that thirty would have had trouble anyway. Lack of tact and sympathy has caused more ministers to be fired than has faithfulness.

I know another church which, not long ago, was almost closed for lack of interest on the part of its members. Now it has all the visible signs of organizational vitality. Not long ago the pastor presented Project Equality to the church's leaders. (Project Equality is the ecumenical program to encourage fair employment, in which persons agree to patronize only those firms that make a special effort to employ people of minority groups.) They turned it down.

Some pastors would have accepted the turndown as a sign that their people were not interested in urban problems and would have either mounted the ramparts to fight for the program or backed off and done nothing more. This pastor responded, "All right. Maybe this isn't the ideal way to solve the problem of poverty and prejudice. What do you think we ought to do about it?" As a result, this church spends more than 10 percent of its budget on a creative inner-city program helping a sister church near the ghetto help people there, and dozens of its people are themselves involved personally in this program.

The fruits of the Spirit are not stubbornness, pride, self-righteousness, and intolerance but "love, joy, peace, patience, kindness, goodness, faithfulness, gentleness, self-control." If faithfulness is seen in this context, there are those called to be pastors who can and do find integrity, faithfulness, and success in the parish ministry.

4.

Priest, Prophet, and Pastor

THE FIRST fact with which we must come to terms is that ever since clergymen quit making tents for a living and started receiving support for their labors in the Lord's vineyard, there has been an inevitable conflict of interest. A great many of the troubles that arise in the relationships between a pastor and his people come from the tendency of the people to view him as a hired hand, and from his resistance to this notion—a resistance that loses some of its force when one hears pastors making noises like union organizers and threatening to strike for higher wages. (In the New Testament it was soldiers who were admonished to be content with their pay!)

Whether the support of the clergy comes from begging person-to-person (as by traveling friars), from taxation (the method of early New England and some European countries today), from the wealth of the church's estates (as in England), or, as is our custom, from voluntary gifts obtained by professional promotional techniques from our parishioners, there is no way to escape entirely the feeling of being "kept." Somebody has described the pastoral role as that of a spiritual prostitute who offers spiritual rather than physical love in return for money. There is more truth in this stereotype than in some others.

This is a problem in every pastor's life. Some compensate by wanting to own their own homes instead of living in a manse. Others decline to accept fees for services. I can remember my own policy of declining some and accepting others, carefully worked out early in my ministry and abandoned piecemeal as my resolution weakened. All of us would like to be in the position of the privileged few who have independent means and can therefore be more forthright than the rest of us in dealing with church trustees.

The only New Testament basis for a paid clergy is found in two obscure references to the " 'laborer deserv[ing] his wages.' " One of these refers to the right to room and board of the Seventy whom Jesus sent out as evangelists, and the other is in the section of First Timothy that speaks about church officers.

Nevertheless, like many institutions of long standing whose antecedents are questionable, the full-time paid clergy seems to be a permanent part of the life of the church. Of course, celibate Roman Catholic priests come a great deal cheaper than Protestant ministers, whose children almost always have the best appetites in town. The exceptions to the rule of a paid clergy are in groups such as the Mormons or the Jehovah's Witnesses, whose ties to one another are cemented in a common attachment to doctrines that only they can accept, and Quakers, whose worship and teaching appeal to people of high intellectual attainments who may be allergic to organizational institutions. It is interesting to note that in parts of the country in which Quakers have become not a "peculiar people" but a church ministering to all sorts and conditions of men, they have defected from the pure teaching of the fathers and have a paid clergy.

There are pragmatic if not theological arguments in favor of the full-time paid clergy. The first is that, presumably, the pastor who is paid a full-time salary can give all his working time to the labors to which God has called him. Sometimes there is an open question as to how much time he owes God and how much he owes the congregation that has also called him, but this is the tension with which he must live. It is in conversations on this subject that churches and ministers are often forced to face quite clearly their convictions as to what the church and ministry are all about.

I am convinced that the exercise which is necessary to separate church members from enough money to support a pastor in this country is the single most important factor explaining the great strength of American religious institutions in contrast to those in the "old countries" across the Atlantic.

In any case, a person who is unable to live in the climate of moral ambiguity occasioned by being expected to be a man of God dependent on the support of fallible human beings in a congregation that is supposed to be committed to the same God but sometimes exhibits the same failings as the pastor—such a person had better find some vantage point like a chair in a theological seminary from which, once the magic word *tenure* is written in the university's book of life, he can hurl all the prophetic thunderbolts he wants to without peril to his income or his conscience.

The theory is that a congregation of God's people calls a man whom it can set apart to exercise his spiritual gifts among them, preaching and teaching God's saving, healing word and fulfilling the role of spiritual leader in the church and community. This is never brought off quite the way it should be. But fortunately, enough of God's Spirit is left in both the ministry and the church that wonderful things do happen as a result. This is why the ordained ministry endures as an institution, why, even in our mad, mod world, some stick it out with optimism and enthusiasm.

The three classic roles

Every clergyman is at times priest, prophet, and pastor. However, for the sake of identifying some of the problems and opportunities of the pastoral ministry, I shall discuss these roles separately as if a clergyman could be one without the others.

I do this realizing that some priests are a great deal more prophetic than some who would like to be classified as prophets. How would you classify Father Groppi, the Roman Catholic priest of Milwaukee who is the city's gadfly and Socrates, bringing nothing except trouble to the establishment until it gives justice to the poor? Wasn't Ezekiel a priest? and Hosea?

Yet, admitting the arbitrariness of trying to dissect the pastoral role into its component parts, it is possible to see these as separate roles, each in its own way providing to many servants of God the three blessings this book is all about: inner integrity, faithfulness to the Christian gospel, and the chance for success in pursuit of some achievable goals.

Priest

A few years ago Father Malone, dean of the Maryknoll Seminary in Ossining, New York, addressed an important Protestant gathering on the goals of the world mission of the Roman Catholic Church. His definition of the goal of mission is the best definition I know of the priestly ministry. Father Malone said, "In Jesus Christ, God has made salvation available to all mankind—those long dead, those alive at any time in history, and all those yet to be born. It is the goal of the church's mission to make that salvation sacramentally present in the midst of every people in every land on earth."

A Protestant would not say it in quite those words, and if he did, he would not mean quite the same thing. But there are Protestant pastors whose vocational goal is very close to this. Neither their call nor their nature is to be militant. They see the Christian life as the stubborn cultivation of the gifts of kindness, compassion, and piety—the last being the source of the first two. They are not given to political activity, and they will tolerate almost any government that will let them hold services. Churches led by men such as these exist in China, Russia, and the Protestant remnants of Spain. There are also many such in our country. They are likely to be despised by prophets, and it is true that many of the cop-outs and timeservers are in this group. Yet it would be and is a grave mistake to conclude that all priestly pastors are cowards and "hireling prophets."

These have a message from God that in their gentler and less bombastic way they persist in repeating. It makes, among others, the following points:

1. If there had been no worshiping community, there would have been no prophets. Even though the Hebrew prophets preached against Israel's sins, unless there had been a covenant, a praying people, a handing-down of the blessed law—and later the gospel—there would have been no sacred soil out of which prophecy, reformation, revival, and renewal could grow. Somebody needs to guard the source of God's life in the world.

2. After all the social battles have been won (if that should ever happen) and everyone can vote, can live in a decent environment, and can have a job if he wants it, all will be lost even then if the people do not have the inner self-discipline to get up and go to work at the job or the moral forbearance to keep their families in one piece and refrain from stealing, violence, and folly. The prophetic dictum of our day that all problems are social and that we need now to convert institutions rather than people is more of a simplification than the old evangelistic doctrine that if everyone would come to Jesus the world would be heaven.

3. George A. Buttrick was right when he said in his book *Christ and Man's Dilemma* that the deepest understanding of the plight of humanity is in three simple facts: The individual knows he is ignorant yet has a deep yearning to know; he knows he is

a sinner yet has a deep yearning to be good; he knows he is mortal yet hungers to live. Only in the church in the midst of the worshiping, learning fellowship can he be convinced of the divine truth to cure his ignorance, receive the divine forgiveness for his sins, and be shown the eternal hope that makes his mortality bearable.

4. It is the vocation of the priestly pastor to recruit, organize, train, and tend the community of the New Covenant, the church. He does this through ministering to people when they gather together and individually in their homes. Most of all, being God's man, he is their fellow sufferer in times of pain and death, their fellow celebrator in times of rejoicing, and the mediator of God's presence by the office he holds and the creed he professes.

Just as there are true and false prophets, there are true and false priests. The temptation of the priest is to be a moral amoeba taking no stands on any issues and, in trying to be all things to all men, winding up as a nothing to everybody. The true priest lets his people know what he thinks about racial prejudice, immorality, public corruption, war and peace; but he lets them know by persistent love rather than by the tactics of "confrontation" which are the strategy of the prophet. He trusts that in the meat grinder of life through which God is putting us, he will bring us face to face with the truth in his time and his way.

The greatest need of the priest is for faith in God and in the means of grace provided by the church. His vocation has always been subject to ridicule. His moral failures are magnified by the exposed position he takes as a teacher of holy living. The current mood of theology dismisses him as "irrelevant." But he is not irrelevant to the people he serves. He can be the bulwark of their shaky marriages, their recourse in time of temptation, their comforter in time of sorrow, and their friend Godward in time of need.

In this role, if one is truly called to it, there is integrity, a scope for faithful obedience to God, and a chance for success in the achievement of some good purposes.

Prophet

The priest's gifts are likely to be faith, hope, and love, and he may lack courage and boldness. On the other hand, the prophet burns with an inner fire that consumes his fear, but he often lacks faith, hope, and love.

The classic prophet is Amos. Even the fact that he is sent from Judah to preach to Samaritan Israelites makes him of purer prophetic stuff because he does not feel for the people to whom he preaches as does Jeremiah, for instance.

Whereas the priest is the minister of God's grace, the prophet is the minister of his wrath, and Amos epitomizes this role. He comes from Judah full of anger and outrage at the injustice and moral iniquity of the establishment at Bethel, the official place of worship of Israel's king. His motivation is all from the inside. God has ignited a fire in his belly. As he has sat by night watching his sheep or worked by day tending his sycamore trees, the thought has burned within him that at this very place where his holy and righteous God is worshiped, people indulge in gross immorality and, infinitely worse, use their power and wealth to exploit the misery of the poor.

There can be only one message—simple, clear, all blacks and whites—God is a holy God who demands justice and right living. The Bethel worshipers have in the very act of worship defied God's judgment. Therefore, God's punishment has already been decreed. There can be no reprieve; no penance will atone for the wrong. God's judgment will be carried out, and Amos is God's messenger.

If a prophet is a classic prophet like Amos, then he cannot be anything but successful. He is answering God's summons. He is faithful to the call. He issues the message loud and clear. So what if he is stoned or banished or imprisoned? His job is done. He has completed the errand for which he was born.

But there just aren't many classic prophets, completely pure in the prophetic role. Jeremiah has been mentioned. Hosea had his hang-ups and could not escape the notion that God's love sometimes takes all the fun out of his wrath. In our American culture there is probably more tolerance of prophets than in any other (with the possible exception of England). However, the tolerance is not in the church, where one might expect to find it, but outside the church. A professor with tenure probably has a greater degree of free speech than any other human being. He can get himself in trouble by doing things that are against the law, for example, conspiring to challenge the authority of the state or swimming in a harbor where the government is preparing to launch a submarine. But he can say about anything he wants.

A prophet who finds himself employed as a parish minister does have problems. Not the least of them is that prophets are usually called upon to travel. I do not know how Amos' boss in Tekoa took to his leaving the orchard and hiking out of the country to prophesy. Maybe he was self-employed—an advantage equivalent to the independent means possessed by some pastors. Anyhow, prophetic pastors often feel moved to go to Washington or Selma or Memphis or some other place where a confrontation is going on, and this gives members of their congregations something to talk about besides their opinions. A lay person always feels ill at ease and overmatched when trying to argue about his religion with the clergy. And never is this harder for him to bear than when he confronts his own minister across a picket line and the minister is carrying a sign which says—in one way or another—that his parishioner is an obstacle in God's way.

Parish ministers with prophetic vocations are always going to be on the edge of trouble—indeed, they always have been. (Consider Martin Luther!) If their object is to turn the existing church into a company made up wholly of militant activists, they are doomed to failure.

But it is not therefore inevitable that prophets cannot be parish ministers. By combining some other gifts with the gift of prophecy, some can be whole, faithful, and successful even within the confines of the "institutional church." Life will not be as tranquil for them as it sometimes is for priests; nor will it be for their parishioners. Nevertheless, wonderful things can happen.

Let us leave Amos as the prototype and pick another prophet, Nathan, from a much earlier chapter of Hebrew history. Nathan was the prophet closest to King David, and a man more complicated but also more skillful than Amos. Let's review his role in the Bathsheba caper. Not only is it a great yarn, but it shows how prophets can survive and still be prophets.

David was strolling on the palace roof high over the city of Jerusalem one day when he spied a lady taking a bath on a patio of an unpretentious house below. Discreet inquiry disclosed that the delectable creature was Bathsheba, wife of Uriah the Hittite, who at that moment was fighting in David's army on a distant battlefield. Being vulnerable to temptation, David summoned the lady to his bedroom. (Did you ever ask yourself how you would really use absolute power if you had it? It certainly increases the opportunity for sinning.) One thing led to another and pretty soon David got a note from Bathsheba announcing that she was pregnant.

Immediately the king had Uriah sent to Jerusalem with messages from the front, but so great was Uriah's zeal for the battle that he would not go and spend the night with his wife before returning but slept with the king's guards instead. This was a great mistake on his part. Failing to cover his hanky-panky in a simple way, David gave instructions that Uriah was to be sent on a suicide mission. After he was killed and Bathsheba had fulfilled a decent but abbreviated period of mourning, the attractive widow received solace as the king's newest wife.

It may be forgiven if we digress long enough to note that she was clever as well as pretty, having the political savvy to have her son Solomon (not the child in this story) made king after David's death over the heads of many other princes his senior.

Well, if ever there was a situation that called for prophecy, this was it. Enter Nathan. If he had been a classic prophet—or one like many parish ministers of our day who are in trouble—he would have brought up this subject on his first visit something like this: "King David, you old lecher, you're a foul, stinking sinner and God will punish you sorely for this offense against his holy laws."

But Nathan was smarter than Amos. In the first place, this was not his first visit to the king. He had been of help to him in earlier times and there was a bond of respect between them.

Second, Nathan knew better than to lower the boom straight off. David had a temper that commanded respect by any prudent man, and Nathan would rather prophesy and live to prophesy another day if he could. He began with a story, as if he were pleading some wronged citizen's cause with the king. It seems that there was a rich man who had thousands of sheep, but the rich man was greedy. So when he needed a lamb to kill for a feast for a visiting dignitary, instead of taking one of his many sheep he took the one little lamb owned by his poor neighbor who kept it as a pet. David reacted the way Nathan knew he would. He was a sympathetic man, and a just one, too, when his emotions were not involved. He exploded. " 'As the LORD lives, the man who has done this deserves to die.' "

With timing that F. Lee Bailey or Clarence Darrow might envy, Nathan was now ready to speak the word: " 'You are the man. . . . because by this deed you have utterly scorned the LORD, the child that is born to you shall die.' "

There it was: judgment and punishment in one quick, clean blow delivered in such a way that David could not escape or evade it. And, in a stroke that prophets often omit, there was an open door to forgiveness after the punishment had been inflicted and acknowledged. " 'The LORD . . . has put away your sin; you shall not die.' " The author thought it worthy of note, also, that after the performance was over Nathan "went to his house." He was not stoned, imprisoned, or banished. Maybe he was later. In those days real prophets were poor risks for life insurance. But at least for this time Nathan survived to prophesy again.

Whether David was from that moment on a changed man may be open to question. For an oriental despot he did quite well to consider at all a moral question in conflict with his own pleasure. But at any rate he was chastened. The fear of God planted some wisdom in him, and he recognized that his kingly authority involved accountability—a lesson that aldermen, selectmen, mayors, and higher officials of our time might learn to their profit and ours.

Parish ministers with strong prophetic vocations stay whole and faithful and successful insofar as they follow the example of Nathan. These are the rules:

First, they establish a relationship of respect, affection, and trust with their parishioners. This assumes that both the minister and the people are trustworthy and that they have enough real religion to make respect possible. It is not necessary that they be lovable, only that they be loving. Is this not the divine command? This relationship cannot be laid on a foundation of dishonesty, and if the essential convictions of minister and laity are so far apart that they are mutually exclusive, then forget it. It is the ministry of Amos or none at all in this instance.

The church is predicated on the assumption that both the minister and the congregation have an ultimate allegiance to Jesus Christ—not just an image of Christ, but a living Spirit—and that they can talk to each other about him and recognize that they are talking about the same Person. If this relationship exists, then communication is possible and both individual growth and common action are possible, on the part of the minister and the people. This may entail a great deal of work on the part of the prophet, which he does not because he thinks it is important but because the people he loves want him to do it—like saying grace at the monthly meeting of the women's society, visiting shut-ins, or even joining the Lions Club.

Second, prophets choose carefully the issues on which they are going to prophesy. One of the few prophets I have known intimately who have actually been sent packing by vote of the church aroused greatest ire in the congregation when he insisted that the confirmation class be received into membership in the church on Palm Sunday evening rather than Maundy Thursday, as was the custom. One of the things prophets have to watch is that God will show them a great many more wrongs that need righting than he wants them to attend to personally. It is all very well to lay one's job on the line if it appears that the church is about to exclude a family because of its color. But the minister's right to run for the school board on the Democratic ticket or absent himself from the parish without announcement ought at least to be a matter of discussion with the Board of Deacons, with a bit of flexibility on the minister's side.

I remember two young ministers who went to Selma.

One went without telling anybody, and his absence was announced by the substitute he got to fill the pulpit for him on Sunday. On the basis of this and many other similar activities it later became necessary for him to leave that parish. The other young pastor took my advice to talk the matter over with his Church Council. He did this, explaining why it was very important to him to participate in this great witness on behalf of those who were being denied their rights as American citizens on account of their race. The upshot of this conversation was that this rather conservative group of middle-class people raised $265 from the parish in a special offering to buy their minister a ticket to Selma and back.

The issue must be important enough to justify the declarative stance of prophecy, and the religious implications of it must be clear enough to make people understand it as a Christian issue. The best way for a prophet to get a one-way ticket elsewhere is to give the impression that he is using the Christian pulpit as a place to peddle his own political opinions, which derive not from Christian ethics but from political ideology. If the issue is obviously of vital importance and can be presented as one about which Christian teaching is not ambiguous, then there are many congregations whose members will hear about it humbly even if it means cost and risk to them personally.

Third, prophets use tact and skill in presenting their prophetic convictions to the congregation, taking into account their people's interests, levels of understanding, and personal feelings of fear or concern. Nathan's story of the rich man and the poor man's lamb is as good an example as one can find. It describes the moral point he wants to make. It is removed far enough from the issue to be free from the emotional burden which the actual case would have to bear. In other words, the moral point is made before the application of it.

It is interesting that *polite* and *politics* seem to be related words. Unfortunately, many who would like to get the church into politics seem totally incapable of getting politics (in the best sense of the word) into the affairs of the church. Among other things, politics is the science of politeness, being kind and considerate to those you are trying to influence for good. (In this connection I am reminded of a wise old Christian who confessed in reference to a particularly crotchety church officer, "I don't love Elder O'Toole any more than it's my Christian duty to love him.")

Fourth, prophets remember that the message of prophetic judgment is never without the elements of hope and love. If the sentence is passed and the punishment decreed and that punishment is the end of all positive values in the life of the hearer, then the actual impact of the message is only on others who may not be guilty —who are usually either not present or talking. In this case there is nothing to do but await the carrying-out of the sentence.

However, this can never be the case with Christ. There may be no hope for Jerusalem, but there is hope for Israel and for humanity. The Christian message must be a gospel (good news), or it is not Christian. It may be very expensive good news (like " 'deny [yourself] and take up [your] cross and follow me' "), but it always has in it the element of the divine grace (" 'Fear not, little flock, for it is your Father's good pleasure to give you the kingdom' "). For a Christian there is never a time when things have gone to such an extreme that nothing can be done. "There is nothing to do except pray," we say. But praying is doing something significant; and when the prayers seem to be of no avail, then there is hoping, which is also significant. Prophecy that leaves the congregation in sackcloth and ashes is much inferior to prophecy that arouses them to do something that ought to be done about injustice or need or personal integrity.

Whether the prophet should try to exercise his ministry within the parish ministry or outside of it depends on his appraisal of the church and the free institutions of society with which the church is so closely involved. If he regards our society as a bastille which needs tearing down so that a better one may be erected in its place, he might pause and ask the question, "Who will build the better society and what will it be like?" The Reign of Terror was hardly an improvement. But in any case the prophetic role is an indispensable part of God's providence, and the vocation of a prophet is one to be accepted with humility and dedication.

There is an important contrast between the prophet of the twentieth century and the biblical prophet. The biblical prophet's chief task was to *say* something. He saw God's hand in history and pointed it out to the people, or God gave him a message and he delivered it. In the twentieth century prophets not only *say* but *do*. Their messages have to do with the "establishment of programs." (Can you imagine Amos at Bethel saying, "God says you've got to establish a government program for distributing shoes to the poor"?) This is at least one mark of progress one can see in human society in the twenty-five hundred years which have intervened. It is now possible for man to think of righting some wrongs himself with God's help rather than relying altogether on the miraculous intervention of the God of wrath against the powerful doers of evil.

Perhaps the epitome of the twentieth-century prophet is Martin Luther King: a man of wholeness and integrity if ever one existed; a man faithful to his dream and his vocation; yes, a successful man as well, although not if you think of his ultimate goals, which were nothing less than the fulfillment of the American dream and the coming of God's kingdom. But in terms of victories won and living seeds planted, his life was one that combined God's purposes with his own and finished some. So he was shot down before he was forty? So was his Master; and I guess things have not changed quite that much yet.

Pastor

In the final chapter of the Gospel of John there is a touching encounter between Peter and the risen Lord. Three times (the same number of times Peter denied him the night he was betrayed) Jesus asked Peter, " 'Do you love me?' " Each time the answer was insistently affirmative. Then, also each time, Jesus commanded Peter, " 'Feed my lambs. . . . Tend my sheep. . . . Feed my sheep.' " This is the biblical origin of the pastoral role. Traditionally, the apostles have been considered as those people appointed by Christ to teach the world the good news and to care for the church as a shepherd cares for his flock.

I know that some will think that "my sheep" means all the people in the world, and there is a sense in which the pastoral vocation has a worldwide reference. John Wesley articulated it when he said, "The world is my parish." But there is a sense in which every pastor is a shepherd to a particular flock, responsible to God for its spiritual welfare, and to it for the manna of God's word.

If the priestly role is the thesis and the prophetic the antithesis, the pastoral role is the synthesis. The pastor must be both priest and prophet, but priest and prophet to a definable people first and then to the rest of the world through them and their life with him in the community of faith and love.

Whereas the priest's primary concern is likely to be the church and its services of worship, and the prophet's compulsion to speak for God rises most often to the top of his consciousness, the pastor is likely to think first on waking of his people. There is a temptation in all three roles. The priest can be so busy with the form of worship that he loses touch with the content; the prophet can hear God's word so loud and clear that he transmits it without translation and the people do not understand; the pastor can be so dependent on the love and appreciation of his people that he falls into the trap of trying to please them rather than God.

The absolute mandate of the pastor is to keep these three commitments in balance and to fulfill all three in the conduct of his ministry. The knowledge of the priest is theology and liturgy; the knowledge of the prophet is theology and ethics; and the knowledge of the pastor is theology and the behavioral sciences since his business is God and people. But a pastor who is complete must combine liturgy with ethics so that human behavior has its roots in worship and its fruits in right living and works of mercy and justice.

As I have observed over the years the cop-outs and

dropouts, the timeservers and the successes and the casualties of our calling, the following characteristics have seemed to me to be present in a person who finds vocational fulfillment in the parish ministry:

1. A talent for performing, and a desire to perform, the work of a pastor: preaching, conduct of worship, pastoral care (which includes both feeding the sheep as individuals and seeing that the sheepfold is kept in repair). Many people enter the ministry so that they will have opportunity to carry on avocations as community leaders, entertainers, artists, psychologists, even arts and crafts instructors. There is nothing wrong with any of these, and there are pastors who fill all these roles and others to perfection. But if they do not like or cannot do what is required and expected of them, they are likely to become either bored or quarrelsome or both.

This is not to say that the pastoral role is not changing or that there are not changes necessary in the expectations of a congregation as to what its pastor should be working at. Nevertheless, the skill to talk over things like this with a congregation is one of the necessary talents of a pastor. A good pastor feels, "I belong here; this is what I was made for," as he listens to the prelude on Sunday morning, or as he leaves the bedside of a hospital patient, or as he begins to put the ideas of a sermon in order and dress them up with good illustrative material.

2. A deep conviction about the truth and importance of religious belief. I call this the "woe is me if I preach not the gospel" syndrome. If a pastor does not have this, he is likely to find his work trivial and insignificant. It is a cliché to say that the good news of God's love in Christ Jesus is either the most important thing in the

world or arrant nonsense. Many pastors who complain about the ministry are among those who have lost their faith because they have read a book by a smart man who says God is dead. Warm piety can be a snare as well as a joy, but it is indispensable to a complete pastor.

3. A love for the church great enough to make the effort to reform it worthwhile. Those who speak of the end of religion and the termination of the life of the church often do so with a yawn. Unless the death of the church is at least as painful a prospect as the loss of a dear friend, one had better not be gainfully employed as the leader of a church. There are many who think the church is so "irrelevant" and corrupt that its loss would have no effect at all on human life or the outcome of history. Of course, they may be right.

To be a pastor, however, one must have the conviction that the church has been sicker than it now is and has got better, and that the main business of the church (worship, Christian teaching, pastoral care, evangelism) is the most important business going on in the world. Many unhappy pastors are earning their salaries maintaining an institution in which they no longer believe. This is hard on them, but it is grossly unfair to their congregations, which still do believe in the church.

4. Acceptance of himself as a human sinner, called by God to serve him, but not himself the Messiah. Many unhappy pastors are miserable because their authority is not immediately accepted and obeyed. They have not learned the lesson that authority, at least for the pastor of a free church, needs to be earned and then exercised with care and good judgment. It is amazing what power can be wielded by those who, like a

woman, have learned "how to let other people have her way." But the dominating, bossy, humorless parson who rules the roost with sarcasm and belligerency will be unsuccessful and unhappy.

5. An appreciation for and empathy with all kinds of people. Pastors are trained how to talk. They are often aggressive "take charge" people. These are both good qualities. But they need to know how to listen too. They need to hear what people are saying when they are not talking, but when they are communicating through the symbols of the eye and the hand. Pastors must know how to sit where the other fellow sits and see things as he sees them. Only from this vantage point can real communication be established. Particularly, pastors need to know how to relate to people unlike themselves: the rich and the poor, people from other countries who hold other faiths. There is a humorous sign we see here and there which says, "I love mankind. It's people I can't stand." This is a common defect in pastors who become casualties or dropouts.

6. An inner integrity great enough to let him exercise the gifts God has given him without being torn apart by rapid shifts in theological climate around him. Many pastors today have an almost childlike faith that the latest word out of the seminaries must be the truth replacing all previously learned lessons, like some latest word from ideological headquarters in Moscow or Rome. The ministry is no job for an ideological chameleon who changes his coloration every time he listens to a different lecture. A pastor needs the talent to be himself, to change when he is really convinced, to do his homework and know what the wise men of his

and earlier days have said, but to make his own ultimate decisions.

There are two parts to this final gift so essential for a pastor to have and to cultivate: The first part has to do with self-appreciation, the basic religious belief in one's vocation, the sense of being called. The second is the ability to be in command of one's powers, the ability to make oneself get up and go to work. Let us look at these in more detail.

Belief in one's vocation is a subtle kind of conviction. It can go astray, as has been noted, when one sees himself as the Messiah. It can go to pieces when one becomes a member of a "school" or a party. Karl Barth once said, "Thank God I'm not a Barthian!" The personal and individual nature of vocation is related to the particular set of gifts bestowed by God on only one person.

When I am invited to give the charge to an ordinand, I frequently tell him to remember David, the shepherd boy, who dared to fight Goliath with his own weapon, the one he knew how to use. Armor, swords, spears, and javelins were the weapons of the soldiery, but when David put on Saul's harness he looked more ridiculous than Don Quixote. He won because he dared to be himself and trusted the sling he was master of.

There are some ministers whose stock in trade is prayer and retreats and cell groups; there are others who are born teachers; there are a few for whom the pulpit is a doorway into the hearts of people to heal and renew and inspire. Some ministers are community organizers (and some who think they are, are not—which could be said of all gifts); and there are those whose genius is to operate one to one in the confessional or the coun-

51

seling room. These things go in and out of style. The popular notion is abroad that at a given time all pastors must be pulpiteers, or counselors, or educators, or reformers. But God did not make it that way. All must preach, conduct worship, counsel, and serve as the chief elder of the church; but all need not do them the same way, and what the pastor does beyond these essentials should be "his own thing."

There is a danger in what is said here. The time when stereopticon slides would draw people out on Sunday nights has gone. (When I read this to my class at Divinity School, the students asked, "What are stereopticon slides?") We do need to heed those who warn against the folly of trying to relate outmoded methods and ideas to a new world that has left them behind. But the gifted pastor has the judgment to know what is worth saving, to stick it out when the reasons presented for change are not convincing enough, and to go beyond what is proposed if it is right.

My father was engaging in "exciting new ministries" forty years ago on a rural seacoast: combining pastoral services with schoolteaching and social work, mixing in medical and dental care when it was needed, organizing house churches (although not calling them that) in towns too small for a full-fledged church, and a dozen other things that some people believe were just thought of since 1960. He did these things because they met the needs of that place and time and were in the spirit of the gospel of Christ, not because they were fashionable or a judgment on more conventional programs elsewhere.

The pastor must be a self-starter. This seems like such a rudimentary and obvious characteristic, but it has to be mentioned because so many pastors fail for lack of it. There are people who cope with life quite acceptably as long as somebody tells them when to get to work, what to do, how to do it, and stands over them to see that they get it done. When these people get into the parish ministry (and they do sometimes), they suffer. Every request from a parishioner, every letter from denominational headquarters, every deadline for a sermon that must be delivered is a cross to bear, a command to be postponed and evaded, another straw on the back of the camel which will ultimately be broken.

Part of the personal wholeness necessary for a pastor is the ability to select—without making people mad and without blowing a fuse from overwork—which tasks are important enough to demand immediate attention, which to put on the secondary list (without forgetting them), and which to decide not to do.

Summary

A pastor is a synthesis of parish priest and prophet, related to and responsible to God for the care of a particular people.

Those who find this vocation personally fulfilling are likely to be people who (1) have a talent for preaching, conducting worship, caring for souls, and bearing rule in Christ's church, and have a desire to do so; (2) are convinced that the good news of God's love in Christ Jesus is not only true but the most important truth in all the treasure-house of the knowledge of mankind; (3) are possessed of a love for the church great enough to make the effort to reform it worthwhile; (4) are blessed with a sense of humor about themselves, convinced of their divine mission but not personally messianic; (5) are outgoing "people who like people"; and (6) have integrity enough to be motivated by their own vocations more than by the theological fads of the day, and self-mastery enough to work without sloth or frantic busyness.

At the extreme right on the spectrum of ministers are priestly pastors who have forgotten the content of religion while tidily conducting the forms of it. These sometimes have little trouble, but often do little good. At the opposite extreme are those pastors whose prophetic zeal is so strong that they chafe at the restrictions placed upon them by any organizational limitation. These often find it difficult, and sometimes impossible, to survive in the pastoral role.

Between these extremes is a wide scope for ministry that allows for personal integrity, religious faithfulness, and some success in the completion of important tasks. The kind of world we live in places great stress and strain on all pastors (as it does on teachers and governors and any others in places of responsibility). It also subjects the pastor to multiplied temptations, magnifying the conflict of interest inherent in his being subsidized by the people he is sometimes commissioned to rebuke in God's name. Every pastor sometimes will ask himself why he ever got into this crazy man's business. But he will usually have an answer, sometimes in the words of the apostles when asked by Christ if they, too, were thinking of leaving him in the days of his unpopularity: " 'Lord, to whom shall we go? You have the words of eternal life.' "

5.

OK—So We Are Middle-class Americans

"MIDDLE CLASS" has become a sneer word almost as widely used as *common* was in the Victorian era. It is a bag into which has been put all that is phony, shallow, smug, materialistic, hypocritical, selfish, snobbish, ostentatious, and empty in American life. If we want to get rid of a notion or a person who disagrees with us, we pin on the label *middle class* and that's the end of the discussion.

The problem of the Protestant pastor is that he is usually of the middle class himself, and most of the people who will be the members and supporters of his church are in the middle class. If the church is Christ's body, Christ is in the awkward position of trying to change the world into the kingdom of God by using the very people who have the most to gain by leaving the world the way it is.

The conundrum is compounded by the fact that the only group in American civilization today on which it is open season for sneering is the middle class, particularly the Anglo-Saxon middle class. Books on the subject abound. Do you recall, for example, *The Man in the Gray Flannel Suit, The Status Seekers,* and *The Organization Man*? If books had been written about Negroes or poor people with the same amount of truth and the same amount of stereotype as these, they would have been banned. And I guess they should be—" 'to whom much is given, of him will much be required.' " I am old enough to remember the contempt with which we viewed imperialistic Englishmen in days before the British Empire was liquidated. It is the nature of everybody to magnify the faults of those who are on top; and it is the nature of those on top to have faults—just as everybody else has faults. However, their faults, because of their greater influence on others, do more harm than do the faults of the poor and the weak.

In what I am trying to say here I do not want to gainsay the obvious truth that if the world does not change voluntarily, it will change violently; nor do I want to gloss over the special troubles that we are in as a nation and as a church because of those sins which have been labeled *middle class* by the critics of our generation.

What I do want to say is that just as the mad, mod

world is the one we've got, so the American middle class is the one we've got. Anybody in the ministry or contemplating it must come to terms with this issue: Is he going to appoint himself the enemy of the middle class to overthrow it and put another class in its place, or is he going to work in and through the middle class for a better church and a better world? If one has chosen the role of overthrower, then I can be of little help to him. That is not to say he may not be right about history and I may be wrong. All I plead for is the same kind of objectivity and openness in dealing with the haves as we are asked to employ in appraising the potentiality of the other blocs in our society.

All this criticism of the middle class results in two equally bad tendencies. On the one hand, it may make us overly defensive so that we become blind to the need for reform, or, on the other hand, we may become so guilt-ridden that we despise ourselves in the same way that Jews or Negroes or the poor in general often despise themselves when they come to believe the sweeping evil generalities that others believe about them.

For instance, take the generation gap, which may or may not be any wider than it always has been. The stereotype is that all parents want their children to grow up just like them to be cocktail-drinking, commuting, conforming, money-making, suburb-living hypocrites. The young people do not want this but cannot tell the adults because this kind of conversation results in shouting; so the youngsters run away and become hippies in order to live a life of honesty in search of true morality and spiritual values. Like all other stereotypes, this one has a grain of truth in it. But also like all other stereotypes, it is an oversimplification.

When a youngster wants to become a missionary or join the Peace Corps and his father blows his stack because he has his heart set on turning the funeral business over to him (or the drygoods business or any other money-making enterprise), there is the classic conflict of youthful idealism versus mature cynicism, and it may very well be described in terms of "false middle-class values."

But when the daughter of a Christian home decides to move in with and share the bed of a male fellow student without benefit of clergy for the duration of college, the objections of her parents may be on biblical grounds, or just because they know more about human nature than she does. If the preservation of the monogamous family is "middle-class morality," it is also Christian ethics, sound psychology, and indispensable to the preservation of an orderly society (as its absence in some strata of society both high and low demonstrates all too clearly). It also needs to be said that monogamy without love is a prison. Obviously, there is a need for clearer and more precise thinking on these matters than we are accustomed to.

The church has always been middle-class

The point has often been made that Jesus and the apostles were poor people and therefore of the proletariat. When compared with people enjoying American affluence in the twentieth century, they were all doubtless below the poverty level. But in their own world they were very much middle-class. As a carpenter Jesus was an independent tradesman, and the fishermen among his disciples owned boats and nets and may even have employed helpers in their business.

This may not be of great significance, but it is a historical fact that, with notable individual exceptions, the church has never made its greatest conquests among the very poor or the very rich—nor among the very bright on university campuses. Ever since Lydia, the cloth seller, opened her home to Paul for the organization of a church in her hometown, women and middle-class people of both sexes have been more receptive to the call to help spread the gospel than people of any other class.

To be sure, there are bad reasons as well as good ones for this. Morality is good for business. People who keep their word get to work on time and pay their bills. Religion—almost any religion—is good for an orderly society. This makes for the abuse of religion and the church.

However, there are good reasons too. Unlike the intelligentsia, who are philosophically inclined and cerebrally motivated and thus often cannot bring themselves to the kind of suspension of argument required by religious faith, the middle classes are likely to be pragmatic and optimistic and find help in a religion that "works."

At any rate, a pastor must be willing to accept and love middle-class people if he is to be effective within the organizational church.

The middle classes are people,
and can be God's troops

The book *God's Frozen People,* by Mark Gibbs and T. Ralph Morton, makes the comment that the greatest untapped reservoir for good in the world is the people who sit in the pews of Christian churches Sunday after

Sunday. They are, it is said, God's frozen assets needing to be thawed out and put to work.

One of the reasons they stay frozen is that their leaders often do not understand them and, even worse, do not begin by recognizing them as persons who have a right to their own particular peculiarities. Programs devised by ministers for action by churches are too often designed with scholars and political activists in mind. It is amazing how many middle-class bank tellers and schoolteachers can be made into scholars and political activists. A Junior Chamber of Commerce type who is chairman of a pastoral committee complained that a sermon he heard by a candidate was a "middle-of-the-road, namby-pamby nothing with no edge to it." But these will always be in the minority of church people. There must be handles to the kingdom of God devised for people who will never attend an adult Bible class or join a march on Washington.

It is good to begin by looking squarely at the "Protestant ethic," the way of life of the middle class. I know no better expression of it than a reply given by an American Mother of the Year to a reporter's question. This mother had raised four sons, all of whom had distinguished themselves conspicuously as benefactors of society. One was a famous surgeon, another was in politics, another had established a business employing hundreds of people, and the other was in a service profession of some sort. "How do you account for the fact that your boys turned out so well?" she was asked. Her reply was quite revealing: "I am a simple woman without a great deal of education, but I wanted my boys to be of use to the world; so I concentrated on teaching them three things. I taught them to pray, to mind their manners, and to work."

Prayer, good manners, and work are out of style in much of the world today. God is dead; so why pray? The way to get things is not by good manners, but by manners so atrocious that they confront, encounter, shock. And work is just a "middle-class compulsion" which we must get rid of in order to enjoy the three-day work week.

Nevertheless, let's take another look. Prayer has been counted out many times before and come back. Good manners do create a style of life that can hold the Christian virtues of gentleness and patience. And all that our friends are saying when they exalt the virtue of work is that Paul was right when he wrote to the Thessalonians: "If any one will not work, let him not eat." Certainly, we can begin with these principles and build on them rather than throw out, by rejection and ridicule, a way of life that has provided both social order and economic productivity for a long time. The spirit of our generation says that every human being is an end in himself. The Protestant ethic says that a human being is best fulfilled if he recognizes himself as related to God and occupies his time in being of use to his fellowmen. Are these beliefs mutually exclusive? I think not. Neither has the whole of the gospel in it. Both are good starts toward the kingdom.

In any case, the most representative lay person in our church is likely to be committed to prayer, good manners, and work at least for the duration of this generation. This means that while he may be willing to consider new insights into theology (realizing that "as for knowledge, it will pass away"), he will not be interested in religion without piety. Therefore, he will expect a minister who himself knows the way to God in prayer.

It means that he may make demands on a pastor regarding bathing, hair cutting, and dress which are out of step with the habits of one who recently has been a student. It will be difficult to teach him that a stinking sweatshirt is a means of grace.

As for work, he finds it confusing to be told, on the one hand, that a third of the people in the world are living at the starvation level and, on the other, that we can produce enough for all in three days a week. But whether or not work is necessary for production of the necessities of life, it is necessary for the fulfillment of the human spirit. Ministry to people who exalt work is to find outlets for their creative gifts. If leisure is to be multiplied, there is no reason why it cannot be usefully spent if one is so inclined.

If the people of our churches are to go out into the world and spend their time, treasure, and talent for God, they must have reasons for doing so which relate to their deepest feelings of what is good and which carry them on vocational paths and through experiences that they find exciting and significant.

Pastors frequently discover that people would rather give money to feed the hungry and join in programs to build housing than support boycotts or pass laws making discrimination a crime. When confronted by this kind of reaction, many a pastor will discourage the programs the people want because they will not support what he regards as the more basic social therapy. The better strategy is to let them "do their thing" and find in doing it the reasons for the more radical approaches later—if indeed they are there.

The identification of secular movements with the will of God is always perilous. We have had a tendency to baptize every war our country has been engaged in and make it a holy crusade. So it was with the Abolitionist movement, the Prohibition movement, the Women's Suffrage movement, and what has been called in our time the Freedom movement. The fact is that although all of these have both noble and ignoble features, all are movements in which Christians have given of themselves from the highest of motives. All of them are also of the stuff of human fallibility, and to make them compulsory for the faithful is a little like the pope trying to keep birth control in the Christian table of sins in a day when it has become a virtue.

Middle class is about out of gas as a sneer word these days because it has lost any precision of content in this connection. Anybody who is going to make it as a pastor is going to have to come to terms with middle-class people. They are the folks in our society likely to be most rigid and resistant to change simply because they have a stake in things as they are. And, let's not kid ourselves, the "outs" would not be so eager for change if they were "in."

Even so, if we can begin where people are and have imagination enough to present the heavenly vision in terms that are relevant to them, we will be surprised at how far they will follow the Lord. These are God's people. They will respond to God's judgment and answer to his love if they are sure they are hearing God's word and not just the pastor's pique.

The honest fact is that just by existing, by the food they produce and the wealth they create out of the earth, the American middle class has a crucial impact on all the other people of the world—an impact perhaps greater than that of any other single tribe in history. What a world this would be if the people of this class became so sure of God's love that they would desire to thank him by serving others! For good and ill they are people—people with all the faults of humanity and some special faults of their own which are magnified because of their great influence. But in the last analysis, I suspect history will turn on whether they accept or reject the vocation which God's providence has thrust upon them. The pastor who persuades them to be God's people will have to love and understand them (as he himself needs love and understanding) if he is to succeed in his mission.

6.

Neither Swinger nor Square

So HERE we are in a world startlingly different in many ways from that we knew as recently as ten years ago, a world in which change seems to be accelerating at geometric rates, a push-button world in which the button most frequently pushed seems to be the panic button. What will be our watchwords for the future? By what stars shall we plot our course?

The basic fact with which churches and pastors have to cope is the growing polarization that is the current characteristic of all main-line Protestant denominations. The church is roughly divided into two groups: the Swingers and the Squares. By nature, swingers are for works while squares are for faith; swingers are for change while squares like things the way they are; swingers want the church politically active on social issues, but squares are more interested in devotional exercises; swingers want to make the future out of whole new cloth, but squares get their guidelines from the past; swingers are likely to be professors or younger pastors, and squares are more likely to be businessmen or older pastors; swingers like situational morality, but squares prefer the Ten Commandments; swingers are likely to contribute a great deal to the church in the way of advice while squares tend more in the direction of money for their contributions. This polarization has resulted in feelings of hostility and anxiety that are found throughout the church.

As this process of polarization goes on, the church assumes the shape of an amoeba getting ready to reproduce by parting in the middle. More and more people are recruited by one side or the other so that the ends get heavier while the middle gets thinner. A very important issue for the church of Christ is whether this process will proceed to a conclusion or whether the main body of the church can be kept together for significant united mission.

Already, some individuals have opted out because the church would not shape up to their ideas of what it ought to be. Some ministers have departed into government service or the Civil Rights movement with the expressed opinion that there is more chance for Christian service there than in the church, and not a few laymen have decided to stay at home Sunday mornings, feeling that they get enough conflict and pressure at work without having to confront them in the church.

Extremists at either pole are not really listening to anybody but themselves. Those on the left are sure that what we know as local churches will be gone in another decade, and national denominations will also be gone. Those on the right want a church that buttresses the status quo in every detail. So, in reality, no church save one it dominates completely will ever satisfy either of these groups.

The Lord provides us with extremists of left and right as counterbalances to each other. There is a true story about a deacon in a northern Connecticut town who remarked to his pastor one day, "I've lived in this town for thirty-one years; seen a lot of changes in my time; voted against every one of them." People like him keep the brakes on to keep us from moving too rashly. As for the prophets at the other extreme, I take comfort from the fact that, contrary to popular opinion, prophets have never been very good at predicting the future. They often have moral insights that we do well to heed, and most changes for the better receive their first impetus from prophets; but the average gypsy palm reader or meteorologist can usually outstrip them in the crystal ball department.

What we have to fear is not so much the development within the church of ecclesiastical counterparts of the radical left and the radical right in the secular world. The great danger to the church and to the world is the arrant self-righteousness of these people, their delusions of infallibility, and their disregard of clear, revealed truth both moral and theological.

When I went to seminary, I was taught to scorn the

man who closed his mind along with his books when he graduated and never had a new idea from that day on. Although I still deplore this attitude, I have lately become just as disenchanted with those latter-day Sophists who do nothing all day except sit around asking one another, "What's new?" I question whether the man who changes his theology every time a new paperback is published is to be preferred over the one who forms his convictions early and sticks to them throughout his life. Neither is doing much thinking for himself.

As Douglas Horton has often said, "There is only one order in the church, the order of the ransomed sinner." Only those who realize that they themselves are "standing in the need of prayer" can relate in any significant way to people in the church who disagree with them. And if anything is true, it is that no party in the church has a monopoly on either virtue or wisdom.

The middle-of-the-road position has often been held in low regard in our society. It is the refuge of fence sitters and compromisers. But at this time in the life of the church it is "where the action really is." It is not a very safe place because one is likely to attract flak from both directions. But if the church of Christ is to have any unity at all, some swingers and squares must sit near enough to the center to hear what is being said on the other side of the aisle.

Meanwhile, be her life long or short, the church has a tradition to live up to and a mission to perform. I see the tradition and the mission in terms of two key words: *liberal* and *reformation*. These words need to be chiseled out of their current setting and cleansed of accumulated accretions to their meanings. But it is worth the effort to do it, for there are no better words to describe the kind of churchmanship which both the tradition and the opportunity of the church of Christ call for in our day.

Reuel Howe, director of the Institute for Advanced Pastoral Studies in Michigan, recently set forth the stance of his school in a newsletter. It is addressed to ministers, but what it has to say is applicable to the whole church.

Many ministers are torn between the radical critics [of the church] on the one hand and conservative, even reactionary, church members on the other. And when they are despondent because of the reactionary conservatism of some of their members, the excessive cynicism of the radical iconoclast seems justified. When ministers think they have to choose between the reactionary and the radical positions, they are inclined to choose the radical view.

There is another position, and one which [I] try to occupy. It is the liberal one. The liberal tries to keep the meanings of the tradition and of contemporary life in dialogue so that the meanings of the contemporary renew the tradition and the meanings of tradition give rootage and perspective to the contemporary.

This is the lasting meaning of the word *liberal:* not another "ism" in theology or politics, but a frame of mind, an attitude that dares to allow room for different points of view within the household of faith. A little over a century ago Abraham Lincoln (who never became a church member because he could not squeeze into the rigid doctrinal confines of the church of his day) said, "Whenever a church will inscribe over its doorway as its entire requirement for membership the two commandments of Jesus: 'Thou shalt love the Lord thy God with all thy heart and soul and mind and strength, and thy neighbor as thyself,' that church will I join with all my heart."

Many communions within the church of Christ have been for many years churches to which Abraham Lincoln could belong. If we have a distinctive mission in these critical times, part of it is to continue that liberal character.

The fundamentalisms of much of the church today do not have to do with rigidity of theological doctrine, but with rigidity of priority in social strategy. We have members who think that war is the greatest danger to human survival and welfare in the world today. Others think that the greatest evil is communism, or racial injustice, or hunger and overpopulation, or anarchy, or immorality, or failure to worship God. Any one of these evils could—and indeed may, if left unchecked—lead to man's ruin in our generation. The great shame of the church is that people interested in fighting one or another of these evils use most of their energy quarreling about which evil is the greatest, and excommunicating those who happen to want to fight a different giant. If the spiritual firepower of the church could be trained outward against all the enemies of mankind instead of inward against one another, then indeed the powers of evil might shake in their shoes.

This kind of liberal spirit can be present only when the inner central loyalty to Jesus Christ and his church transcends the peripheral loyalty to a party or a business, or even to a movement or a cause; and only among those who really believe that God dwells in all who sincerely confess Christ Jesus as God's Son and are willing to accept one another as brethren and entrust the future to God.

Let me cite an example: Bill Feaster was a person who would be described in Gabriel Fackre's frequently used words, "A free man in Christ." Bill grew up in a parsonage. He was a happy, outgoing lad with his father's sharp wit, his mother's good looks, and plenty of brainpower of his own. He went to Harvard University and Harvard Divinity School. This really should have drained all the religion out of him, but it didn't. While at the divinity school his chief interest was biblical studies in the original languages.

Then he took a job as assistant pastor at the old downtown Center Church in New Haven. While there he found that his openhearted friendliness and deep compassion made him a natural counselor. He also became interested and involved in the Freedom movement in the city, and with his friends he participated in the March on Washington and the Pilgrimage to Selma.

Then, much to the delight of his father, who was beginning to wonder if his son would ever be interested in anything but Greek verbs, he fell in love with an army nurse. One thing led to another and soon Bill was an army chaplain. One day in Vietnam his leg was hit by shrapnel and was badly shattered. Waving the medics off, he crawled around comforting the other wounded and the dying. Then, at last, he was taken to a hospital in Saigon, where a few weeks later he died, the first Protestant chaplain to die in Vietnam of wounds suffered in battle.

Bill Feaster loved the church, and in my opinion he is an example of what the church at its best is all about—not because he went to Selma or to Vietnam (although some of his friends in each place thought he was a traitor to go to the other) but because his conscience was the property of Jesus Christ alone, and he followed that loyalty in loving service to people through the church to all the world.

There is a church covenant first used in Salem, Massachusetts, more than three centuries ago which is enjoying a small revival these days because of its brevity and inclusiveness. I propose it as an expression of the inclusiveness of the contemporary church: "We covenant with the Lord and one with another and do bind ourselves in the presence of God, to walk together in all his ways, according as he is pleased to reveal himself to us in his blessed word of truth."

The other word that we should lay to heart as we seek to cope with our mad, mod world is *reformation*. I set this word in contrast to another word very popular today, namely, *revolution*. When *revolution* is used to mean rapid change, it is a proper description of the present state of the church and the world. But this is not the connotation it usually receives. To be a revolutionary is to invest oneself with a license to destroy, in the often unjustified confidence that one has the competence to build something better in place of that which he has destroyed.

A fine house on our street was recently marked for destruction to make room for a parking lot. Thus, every small boy in the neighborhood had a license to throw stones through its windows, to foul its floors and walls, and to remove doorknobs and other attractive baubles. The delight of many current revolutionaries is like the delight of these small boys. What a feeling of power one has as a wrecker! But adults ought to know better.

Every generation needs wreckers to remove the debris of the past and builders to create the structures of the future. But our generation has far more wreckers than are needed simply because it is much easier to wreck than to build. They stand like blind Samson between the pillars of every institution of our civilization—religious, political, commercial, moral—ready to bring it down with the naïve self-assurance that what they build will be better, forgetting that like Samson they will be buried in the rubble along with their foes.

Listen, once more, to Reuel Howe:

There will always be a place in the city, the suburb, and rural areas for congregations made up of people who, together as well as individually, recognize themselves as servants of Christ. His spirit animates and directs them: they gather to be with Him and each other, to break bread in His memory and to be instructed by Him: they disperse to their places in the world to do their jobs in ways that give witness to their primary loyalty to Him. The "Special" Ministries of our time will emerge out of, and need the context of, the dialogue between the meanings of tradition and contemporary life.

We believe, therefore, in the ministry of the local congregation wherever it exists, as long as its members live the Gospel in creative tension with its total environment. . . . We believe that the form of the Church must and will change, but always in response to the vitality that gave it original existence. That vitality, the Holy Spirit, will speak both through the Church and through the world in the midst of which the Church is set and to which it is sent.

The relationship between the existing churches and the so-called special ministries needs reemphasis. I venture to guess that in this regard never in the course of human events have so few been so ungrateful to so many. We must resist the temptation to assume that all the issues are black and white, and that all the bad guys are on the other side. This applies to radicals as well as to conservatives. The institutions of our day are not perfect, but they took a long time to build and are better than any others that preceded them. Therefore, the shortest way to improvement is reformation rather than total destruction and rebuilding.

The symbol of the ship has long been cherished by the people of God. It began with the ark. Somebody has said that it is as true of today's church as of the ark that only the raging sea outside makes one able to endure the smell inside. Be that as it may, the church, like the seagoing vessel, has changed a great deal through the years. The seal of the World Council of Churches shows a ship like a Phoenician galley of the kind in which Paul was wrecked several times.

Our present time finds the church in a situation very similar to that of ships during the nineteenth century. Sails were going out and steam engines were coming in. But sails were by then developed to their ultimate efficiency and steam engines were rudimentary, unreliable, even dangerous. The conservatives would not have an engine aboard a ship—except maybe a little one to use in weighing anchor and hoisting sails. The radicals were all for chopping down the masts and trusting to steam alone in spite of the risks involved.

Neither the radicals nor the conservatives won that argument. For many years the ships that plied the Atlantic carried both sail and steam. These were not very pretty ships compared with the gorgeous clippers they replaced or the steamships which followed. But they got the job done and provided the experience which led to the *Queen Elizabeth,* the *Nautilus,* and the *Savannah.*

So let it be with the church of our generation.

One thing is sure: Neither the squares nor the swingers are likely to have things all their own way, and probably that's good too.

Let the squares continue to improve as best they can the tested methods of the past in which they believe while the swingers continue to experiment with new ones in which they believe. So what if the old methods do not work quite as well as they did and the new ones have produced more promises than successes so far? If we can remember that the Captain of the ship is Christ, I for one believe that our future will be better together than if one party or another should strike out in its own little whaleboat.

The swingers need the squares and vice versa. Of all the labors to which one might give himself in this mad, mod world, few can be more important than trying to embellish the letter to the Galatians so that it might say, "There is neither Jew nor Greek, there is neither slave nor free, there is neither male nor female, *there is neither swinger nor square;* for you are all one in Christ Jesus."

A Note About the Author

Nathanael M. Guptill is minister of the Connecticut Conference of the United Church of Christ. In this capacity he has pastoral oversight of 290 churches and 350 ministers. He has held almost every type of job open to an ordained minister. He served as pastor of several churches; as field work director, assistant professor of church administration, and lecturer on the Christian ministry at Andover Newton Theological School; as national co-secretary of the United Church of Christ; and as director of the Council for Church and Ministry of the United Church of Christ.

Mr. Guptill received the B.A. and honorary D.D. degrees from Colby College and the B.D. from Andover Newton Theological School.

He is the author of three previous books and of numerous pamphlets and articles in religious journals. For many years he was a staff correspondent for the *Christian Century* and for three years served as editor of the *Minister's Quarterly*.